onl

best email

jokes

of the last

century

Geraldine Flower Publications
London

1

From the editor:

Don't they drive you mad all those 'fun' emails landing on your PC? The graphic that takes forever to load — only to find it is an angel or a teddy bear asking you to smile! Pleeeease!!

All those terrible lists. Who compiles them? Who are these Useless-Facts Junkies? Pages and pages to print. You can't bear it, but maybe — just maybe — there is a really funny twist at the end to make you laugh, like "Questions most feared by men". I have included a few lists here, as examples of the genre and the only ones that raised a smile for me.

And what about the supposed True Stories? Mostly very long, very boring, old urban myths that you were almost(?) fooled by years and years ago. You will find a few — The Irish Bank Robbers is my favourite. I have not included Kidney Stealing or the resurrected bunny rabbit — you, the reader, are saved!

The jokes just keep landing: those old chestnuts where you know the original version was much funnier, if only you could remember it! I am looking forward to loads more new jokes for the next edition of "Only the Best Emails". Meanwhile, my good friends, please keep sending them and extra special thanks to Lesley for her contributions.

Editor   www.jokes-by-email.net

contents:

Subject: Aussie Sport

A keen fan was at the Australian Rules Football League Grand final and he came across a man with an empty seat beside him.

He said, "Excuse me, mate, is that seat taken?" The man in the seat said, "No mate, go for your life."

The man was incredulous. He couldn't believe his luck. "Who would be so daft as to have a great seat like this at the grand final and not use it?" he asked.

"Well mate," the man seated said, "it's my seat. I used to come with my wife, but she passed away and this is the first grand final that I've been to without her."

The stranger said, "I'm sorry mate, but isn't there anyone you could have brought with you......a friend or a neighbour?"

"No," said the man, "they're all at the funeral."

Subject: Presidential Clock

Ashley walked into the White House for the first day of her internship and was greeted by the President. After a tour, he asked, "Would you like to see the Presidential Clock?"

Ashley got suspicious and said, "I've heard certain things about you, Mr President, and I don't think that would be a smart idea."

"Nonsense," said the President. "It's just a clock."

Ashley reluctantly agreed. The President led her to an empty Oval Office, closed the door, dropped his pants and pulled it out.

In a reproving tone, Ashley said, "That's not the Presidential clock; it's the Presidential cock."

The President responded, "Ashley, honey, put a face and two hands on it, and it's a clock."

Subject: The Chicken and The Horse

Two animals, a horse and a chicken, live on a farm on the coast. One day the two friends are out walking along the beach when the horse falls in some quicksand. The chicken rushes back, jumps into the farmer's BMW, drives over to the horse, throws him a rope, drives off and pulls him out.

A few days later, the friends are out again and this time the chicken falls into the quicksand. The horse looks down, sees his friend in trouble and says, "Look, grab onto what's hanging between my legs and I'll pull you out."

The chicken does as he's told and the horse pulls him out.

The moral of the story is: "You don't need a BMW to pull chicks if you're hung like a horse."

Subject: Modern technology

A threesome comprising an American, a German and a Japanese are playing golf. At the 3rd hole, they hear a phone ring. The American excuses himself, puts his left thumb to his ear, his left pinky finger to his mouth, and proceeds to have a telephone conversation. When he is done, he looks at the other two and says, "Oh, this is the latest American technology in cellular phones. I have a chip in my thumb and one in my pinky and the antenna is in my hat. Great stuff eh?"

They continue their game until the 9th hole when, again, they hear a phone ring. The German tilts his head to one side and proceeds to have a conversation with someone in German. When he finishes, he explains to the other two that he has the latest in German technology cell phones. "A chip in my tooth, a chip in my ear and the antenna is inserted in my spine. Ach, the wonders of German superior know-how!"

At the 13th hole, a phone rings again and this time, the Japanese fellow disappears into some>

>nearby bushes. The German and the American look at each other and then walk over and peer into the bushes. In the middle of the bushes is the Japanese fellow, squatting with his pants down around his ankles, and a roll of toilet paper shoved up his behind. "What on earth are you doing?" asks the American. The Japanese fellow looks up and replies, "Waiting for a fax."

Subject: The simple ones are often the best!

From the Churdown Parish Magazine:

Would the Congregation please note that the bowl at the back of the Church, labelled For the Sick, is for monetary donations only.

Subject: The Lone Ranger

The Lone Ranger and Tonto are sitting in a bar
having a beer. A cowboy walks in and says, "Who
owns the big white horse outside?"

The Lone Ranger stands up, hitches his gun belt,
and says, "I do...Why?"

The cowboy looks at the Lone Ranger and says, "I
just thought you'd like to know your horse is about
dead outside!"

The Lone Ranger and Tonto rush outside and sure
enough, Silver is ready to die from heat
exhaustion. The Lone Ranger gets the horse water
and soon Silver is feeling a little better. The Lone
Ranger turns to Tonto and says, "Tonto, I want
you to run around Silver for a little while and see
if you can create enough of a breeze to cool him
down some more."

Tonto says, "Sure Kemosabe", and takes off
running circles around Silver.>>>

>Not able to do anything else but wait, the Lone Ranger returns to the bar to finish his beer.

A few minutes later another cowboy struts into the bar and asks, "Who owns that big white horse outside?"

The Lone Ranger stands again, and claims, "I do....What's wrong with him this time?"

The cowboy looks him in the eye and says, "Nothing, but you left your 'injun runnin'!"

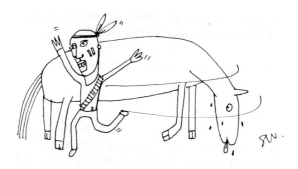

Subject: Three Couples

Three couples, an elderly couple, a middle-aged couple and a young newylwed couple wanted to join a church.

The pastor said, "We have special requirements for new parishioners. You must abstain from having sex for two weeks."

The couples agreed. At the end of the two weeks they returned.

The pastor went to the elderly couple and asked, "Were you able to abstain from sex for the two weeks?" The old man replied, "No problem at all, Pastor." "Congratulations. Welcome to the church!" said the pastor.

The pastor then went to the middle-aged couple and asked, "Well, were you able to abstain from sex for the two weeks?" The man replied, "The first week was not too bad. The second week I had sleep on the couch for a couple of nights, but,>>

>>yes, we made it." "Congratulations. Welcome to the church!" said the pastor.

The pastor then went to the newlywed couple and asked, "Well, were you able to abstain from sex for two weeks?" "No, Pastor, we were not able to go without sex for the two weeks," the young man replied sadly.

"What happened?" enquired the pastor. "My wife was reaching for a can of paint on the top shelf and dropped it. When she bent over to pick it up, I was overcome with lust and took advantage of her right there."

"You understand you will not be welcome in our church," stated the pastor.

"We know," said the young man, "We're not welcome at Do-It-All anymore either."

Subject: Bar joke

Bloke walks into a bar and sits down next to this good-looking girl and starts looking at his watch. The girl notices this and asks him if his date is late.

"No", he replies, "I've just got this new state-of-the-art watch and I was just about to test it."

"What does it do?" asks the girl.

"It uses alpha waves to telepathically talk to me."

"What's it telling you now?"

"Well, it says you're not wearing any knickers."

"Ha, well it must be knackered then, cos I am!"

"Damn thing, must be an hour fast."

Subject: Yet another Little Old Lady

A little old lady goes to the doctor and says, "Doctor, I have this problem with gas, but it really doesn't bother me too much. They never smell and are always silent. As a matter of fact I've farted at least 20 times since I've been here in your surgery. You didn't know I was farting because they didn't smell and are silent."

The doctor says, "I see. Take these pills and come back to see me next week."

The next week the little old lady goes back. "Doctor", she says, "I don't know what the hell you gave me, but now my farts — although still silent — stink terribly."

"Good", the doctor said, "Now that we've cleared up your sinuses, let's work on your hearing."

Subject: Three Mice

Three mice are sitting at a bar in a pretty rough neighborhood late at night trying to impress each other about how tough they are.

The first mouse pounds a shot of scotch, slams the glass onto the bar, turns to the second mouse and says, "When I see a mousetrap, I lie on my back and set it off with my foot. When the bar comes down, I catch it in my teeth, bench press it twenty times to work up an appetite, and them make off with the cheese."

The second mouse orders up two shots of sour mash, pounds them both, slams each glass into the bar, turns to the first mouse, and replies, "Yeah, well when I see rat poison, I collect as much as I can, take it home, grind it up to a powder and add it to my coffee each morning so I can get a good buzz going for the rest of the day."

The first mouse and the second mouse then turn to the third mouse. The third mouse lets out a long sigh and says to the first two, "I don't have time for this bullshit. I gotta go home and fuck the cat."

Subject: Proverbial Essex girl

An Essex girl and an Irish guy are in a bar when the Essex girl notices something strange about the wellies the Irish guy's wearing.

She says to him, "Scuse me mate, I ain't being funny or nuffink, but why does one of your wellies have an L on it, and the uvver one's got an R on it?"

So the Irish guy smiles, puts down his pint of guinness and replies, "Well, Oim a little bit tick you see. The one with R is for me rooight foot and the one with the L is for me left foot."

"Cor blimey!" exclaims the Essex girl, "So THAT's why me knickers 'ave got C&A on them!"

Subject: Isolation experiment

A team of sociologists have planned an experiment in isolation. They send an American, a Frenchman and a Japanese man to a deserted island, and arrange to come back and pick them up in a year's time to see how they have adapted. The sociologists leave, and the three men decide to split up the tasks among themselves.

"I'm an engineer", says the American, "so I'll handle building a shelter." He turns to the Frenchman and says, "You French are pretty good cooks. Why don't you handle the cooking?" The Frenchman agrees, and the American turns to the Japanese man, "That leaves you to organise the supplies", he says. The Japanese man agrees and each man sets about his tasks.

A year passes, and the sociologists return to see how the men have done. They expect to find three desperate men, unhappy with having to live on the island, but instead find a huge wooden house with verandas and porches and balconies. The American comes to greet them, and when they express their surprise about the house he just shrugs and says, "Yeah, well I had a lot of raw>>

17

>>materials so I kind of went to town and did the place up." The team is amazed. They are shown inside to the kitchen where they're greeted with the most wonderful smell of delicious food. The Frenchman sees their surprise and just shrugs, "I had lots to work with", he says. "This island has loads of edible herbs and plants." The team sits down to eat and are about to start when one of them enquires about the Japanese man.

"Oh, we don't know what happened to him", explains the American. "He ran off into the woods to sort out the supplies and hasn't been seen since." They all agree they should find the man, and a search party is organised.

They make it about 100 yards into the woods, when the Japanese man jumps out from behind a tree, stark naked with peacock feathers sticking out his arse, shouting: "SUPPLIES!"

Subject: The Priest and The Frog

One fine, sunny morning, a priest took a walk in the local forest. He was walking by a small stream when, sitting on a nearby toadstool, he noticed a sad-looking frog.

"What's wrong with you?", asked the priest.

"Well," said the frog, "the reason I am so sad on this fine days is because I wasn't always a frog."

"Really", said the priest, "can you explain?"

"Once upon a time I was an 11-year-old choirboy at your very church. I too was walking by this stream when I was confronted by the wicked witch of the forest. 'Let me pass' I cried, but to no avail. She called me a cheeky little boy and with a flash of her wand, turned me into the frog you now see before you."

"That's an incredible story!", said the priest. "Is there no way of reversing the witch's spell?" >

>> "Yes," said the frog. "It is said that if a nice kind person would pick me up, take me home, give me food and warmth and a good night's sleep, I will wake up as a boy again."

"Today's your lucky day!" said the priest, and forthwith picked up the frog and took him home. He gave him lots of food, placed him by the fire to warm, and at bedtime put the frog on the pillow beside him. And, lo and behold! Miracle of miracles! For, when he awoke the next morn, there was the 11-year-old choirboy beside him in bed.

And that, your Honour, is the case for the Defence.

Subject: Doctor's appointment

A couple, both 67, went to a sex therapist's surgery. The doctor asked, "What can I do for you?" The man said, "Will you watch us have sexual intercourse?"

The doctor looked puzzled, but agreed. The doctor examined them and then directed them to disrobe and proceed with intercourse. When the couple finished, the doctor re-examined them and advised the couple, "There's nothing wrong with the way you have intercourse." He then charged them $32.

This happened several weeks in a row. the couple would make an appointment, have intercourse with no apparent problems, other than the lack of vigour which is to be expected in 67-year-olds. Then they would get dressed, pay the doctor, and leave.

Finally, after almost two months of this routine, the doctor asked, "Just what exactly are you trying to find out?"   >>>>>>>>

>>>The old man said, "Oh, we're not trying to find out anything. It's just that she's married and we can't go to her house. I'm married, so we can't go to my house. The Holiday Inn charges $60. The Hilton charges $78. We do it here for $32 and I get $28 back from Medicaid."

Subject: Best Comeback Line Ever

Police arrested Malcolm Davidson, a 27-year-old white male, resident of white Plains, NY, in a pumpkin patch at 11.38 pm Friday. Davidson will be charged with lewd and lascivious behaviour, public indecency, and public intoxication at the County Courthouse on Monday.

The suspect allegedly stated that as he was passing a pumpkin patch, he decided to stop. "You know, a pumpkin is soft and squishy inside, and there was no-one around for miles. At least I though there wasn't," he stated in a phone interview from the County Courthouse jail.

Davidson went on to state that he pulled over to the side of the road, picked out a pumpkin that he felt was appropriate to his purposes, cut a hole in it, and proceeded to satisfy his alleged 'need'. "I guess I was just really into it, you know?" he commented with evident embarrassment.

In the process, Davidson apparently failed to notice the White Plains police car approaching and was unaware of his audience until Officer Brenda Taylor approached him. >>>

>> "It was an unusual situation, that's for sure," said Officer Taylor. "I walked up to (Davidson) and he's.... just working away at this pumpkin."

Taylor went on to describe what happened when she approached Davidson. "I just went up and said, 'Excuse me sir, but do you realise that you are screwing a pumpkin? He got real surprised, as you'd expect, and then looked me straight in the face and said, 'A pumpkin!? Damn.....is it midnight already?'"

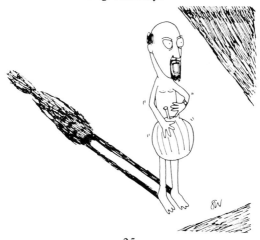

Subject: Lights out

Jane was becoming frustrated with her husband's insistence that they have sex in the dark. Hoping to free her husband from his inhibitions, during a passionate session, she flipped on the lamp, only to discover a cucumber in his hand.

"Is THIS what you've been using on me for the past five years?"

"Honey, let me explain...."

"Why you sneaky bastard!", she screamed. "You impotent son of a bitch."

"Speaking of sneaky," he interrupted, "maybe you'd care to explain our three kids!!!!"

Subject: Little Lucy and Tiddles the Cat

Little Lucy went out into the garden and saw her
cat Tiddles lying on the ground with its eyes shut
and its legs in the air. She fetched her father to
look at Tiddles, and, on seeing the cat, he said, as
gently as he could, "I'm afraid Tiddles is dead,
Lucy."

"So why are his legs sticking up in the air like
that, Daddy?" asked Lucy, as she fought back the
tears.

At a loss for something to say, the father replied,
"Tiddles' legs are pointing straight up in the air so
that it will be easier for Jesus to float down from
above and grab a leg and lift Tiddles up to
Heaven."

Little Lucy seemed to take Tiddles death quite
well. Two days later, however, when her father
came home from work, Lucy had tears in her eyes
and said, "Mummy almost died this morning."
Fearing something terrible had happened the >>>

>> father shook the girl and shouted, "What do you mean, Lucy? Tell Daddy."

"Well", mumbled Lucy, "soon after you left for work this morning I saw Mummy lying on the floor with her legs in the air and she was shouting, 'Oh Jesus!!!! I'm coming, I'm coming!!!' and if it hadn't been for the milkman holding her down, she would definitely have gone, Daddy."

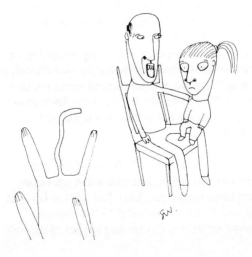

Subject: Choking on a Hamburger

Two men from Texas were sitting at a bar when a young lady nearby began to choke on her hamburger. She gasped and gagged, and one Texan turned to the other and said, "Hell, that little gal is havin' a bad time. I'm gonna go over there and help."

He ran over to the young lady, held both sides of head in his big Texan hands, and asked, "Kin ya swaller?" Gasping, she shook her head, "No". He asked, "Kin ya breathe?". Still gasping, she again shook her head, "No". With that, he yanked up her skirt, pulled down her panties and licked her on the butt. The young woman was so shocked that she coughed up the piece of hamburger and began to breathe again.

The Texan sat back down with his friend and said, "Ya know, it's sure amazin' how that hind-lick manoeuvre always works."

Subject: Superman

Superman was feeling bored after a long stint of no crime fighting, so he called Batman to ask if he wanted to go to a club and pick up some girls. Batman said Robin was ill and he had to look after him.

A little disappointed, Superman called Spiderman to see if he fancied a few beers, but Spiderman told him he had a date with Catwoman.

As a last resort, superman flew over to Wonder Woman's apartment to see if she was free. As he landed on the balcony, he saw Wonder Woman naked on the bed with her legs spread wide open.

Superman thought to himself, "I'm faster than a speeding bullet, I could go in, have sex and be out of there before she knew what was happening!" So, with that, he was off like a shot.

Meanwhile, on the bed, Wonder Woman says, "Did you hear anything?" "No" replies the Invisible Man, "but my ass hurts like hell!"

Subject: Irish humour

Aer Ireland Flight 101 was flying from Heathrow
to Dublin one night, with Paddy the pilot, and
Shamus the co-pilot. As they approached Dublin
airport, they looked out the cockpit window.

"B'jeesus", said Paddy, "will ye look at how fookin
short dat runway is."

"You're not fookin kiddin, Paddy", replied
Shamus. "Dis is gonna be one a' the trickiest
landings you're ever gonna see", said Paddy.

"You're not fookin kiddin, Paddy" replied Shamus.

"Roight, Shamus, when I give de signal, you put
de engines in reverse", said Paddy.

"Roight, Oi'll be doing dat", replied Shamus.

"And den ye put de flaps down straight away",
said Paddy.

"Roight, Oi'll be doing dat", replied Shamus. >>

>> "And den ye stamp on dem brakes as hard as ye can," said Paddy.

"Roight, Oi'll be doing dat," replied Shamus.

"And den ye pray to de Mother Mary with all a'your soul," said Paddy.

"Oi be doing dat already," replied Shamus.

So they approached the runway with Paddy and Shamus full of nerves and sweaty palms. As soon as the wheels hit the ground, Shamus put the engines in reverse, put the flaps down, stamped on the brakes and prayed to Mother Mary with all of his soul.

Amidst roaring engines, squealing of tyres and lots of smoke, the plane screeched to a halt just centimetres from the end of the runway, much to the relief of Paddy and Shamus and everyone on board.   >>>

>> As they sat in the cockpit regaining their composure, Paddy looked out the front window and said to Shamus, "Dat has gotta be de shortest fookin runway I have EVER seen in me whole life."

Shamus looked out the side window and replied, "Yeah, Paddy, but look how fookin wide it is."

Subject: The Doctor's Surgery

A woman is in her doctor's surgery and suddenly shouts out, "Doctor, kiss me."

The doctor looks at her and says that it would be against his code of ethics to kiss her.

About 20 minutes later the woman again shouts out, "Doctor, please, kiss me just once."

Again he refuses, apologetically, but says that as a doctor he simply cannot kiss her.

Finally, another 15 minutes pass, and the woman pleads with the doctor, "Doctor, Doctor, please kiss me just once."

"Look", he says, "I am sorry. I just CANNOT kiss you. In fact, I probably shouldn't even be shagging you!"

Subject: The Mating Bull

A man takes his wife to the stock show. They start heading down the alley where the bulls are exhibited. They come up to the first bull and his sign states: "This bull mated 50 times last year." The wife turns to her husband and says, "He mated 50 times in a year, you could learn from him."

They proceed to the next bull and his sign states: "This bull mated 65 times last year." The wife turns to her husband and says, "This one mated 65 times last year. That is over five times a month. You can learn from this one also."

They proceed to the last bull and his sign says: "This bull mated 365 times last year." The wife's mouth drops open and she says, "Wow! He mated 365 times last year. That is ONCE A DAY!!! You could really learn from this one."

The husband turns to his wife and says, "Go up and enquire if it was 365 times with the same cow?"

Subject: Little Johnny at School

Little Johnny was sitting in his second grade class and his teacher, Miss Parsons, was asking questions about mathematics and logic.

"Johnny, if there were five crows sitting on a fence and I shot two of them, how many would be left?"

"None."

"The correct answer is three, Johnny."

"Yeah, but if you shot two, no way would those other crows hang around."

"Well, Johnny, that's not the answer I was looking for, but I like the way you think."

"Miss Parsons, may I ask you one?"

"Sure, go ahead."

"If there are three women eating ice cream cones, and one kind of takes bites out of hers, another one licks hers, and the other one sucks on hers, which one is married?"

After some thought, "Well, I would say the one who sucks hers."

"No, it's the one with the wedding ring, but I like the way you think."

Subject: Mona Lisa email as screen saver

Here's a sample of one of those clever graphic emails that take a while to load, but worth the effort. Mona Lisa gazes mysteriously from the screen; when you press the space bar she exposes her breasts for as long as you hold the space bar down.

37

Subject: The Bear and The Rabbit

There's a Bear and a Rabbit in the woods and they
come across a Golden Frog. They think this is an
amazing discovery and they are even more amazed
when the Golden Frog talks to them. The Golden
Frog admits that he doesn't often meet animals or
people, but when he does he gives them six
wishes. He tells them they can each have three
wishes.

The Bear immediately asks that all the other bears
in the forest be female. The Golden Frog grants
the wish at a stroke.

The Rabbit, after thinking for a while, asks for a
crash helmet and one instantly appears, which he
places on his head.

The Bear is surprised at this, but carries on with
his next wish. He asks that all the bears in the
neighbouring forests be female as well, and Thus,
it is so!   >>>

>> The Rabbit then wishes that he could have a motorcycle. It appears before him and he climbs on board and starts revving the engine. The Bear cannot believe it. He remarks to the Rabbit that he has wasted two wishes that he could of had for himself.

Shaking his head, he makes his final wish, that all the other bears in the world be female as well. The Golden Frog replies that it has been done, and they both turn to the Rabbit for his last wish.

The Rabbit revs up the engine of his new motorcycle and thinks for a second, then says, "I wish for the Bear to be gay!" — and promptly roars off as fast as he can!

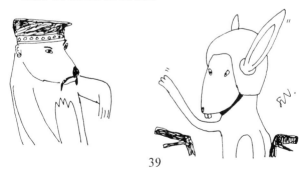

Subject: The Italian Who Went to Malta

Must be read with an Italian accent!

One day ima gonna Malta to bigga hotel. Ina morning I go down to eat breakfast. I tella waitress I wanna two pissis toast. She brings me only one piss. I tella her I want two piss. She say go to the toilet. I say you no understand, I wanna to piss onna my plate. She say you better no piss onna plate, you sonna ma bitch. I don't even know the lady and she call me sonna ma bitch.

Later I go to eat at the bigga restaurant. The waitress brings me a spoon and knife, but no fock. I tella her I wanna fock. She tell me everyone wanno fock. I tell her you no understand, I wanna fock on the table. She say you better not fock on the table, you sonna ma bitch. So I go back to my room inna hotel and there is no shits onna my bed. I call the manager and tella him I wanna shit. He tell me to go to toilet. I say you no understand, I wanna shit on my bed. he say you better not shit onna bed, you sonna ma BITCH.   >>>

40

>> I go to the checkout and the man at the desk say, "Peace on you." I say, "Piss on you too, you sonna ma bitch, I gonna back to Italy."

Subject: The Chicken and the Egg

The chicken and the egg were lying in bed, smoking a cigarette and enjoying post-coital sex.

The chicken says to the egg, "Well that solves that one then."

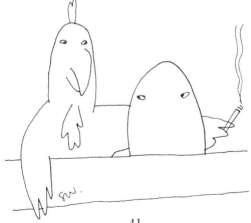

41

Subject: The Affair

A man and his secretary are having an affair, so one afternoon they get a motel room and have strenuous sex. He's not used to the pace, so he falls asleep afterwards and doesn't wake up until about 8.30 that evening, at which time he realises it's late and he has to get home.

He says to his secretary, "Quick! While I get dressed, you take my shoes outside and drag them around through the grass and mud." Puzzled the secretary complies.

When the man gets home about 9.30, his wife confronts him and asks where he's been.

The man says, "I cannot lie to you. I spent the better part of the day doing my secretary in a motel room, then I fell asleep, woke up later, and came right home."

The wife looks down at his shoes and says, "You lying bastard, you've been out playing golf again!"

Subject: Treat me like a woman

On a transatlantic flight, a plane passes through a severe storm. The turbulence is awful, and things go from bad to worse when one wing is struck by lightning. One woman in particular loses it. Screaming, she stands up in the front of the plane. "I'm too young to die!" she wails. Then she yells, "Well, if I'm going to die, I want my last minutes on earth to be memorable! I've had plenty of sex in my life, but no one has ever made me really feel like a woman! Well, I've had it! Is there ANYONE on this plane who can make me feel like a WOMAN???"

For a moment there is silence. Everyone has forgotten their own peril, and they all stare, riveted, at the desperate woman in the front of the plane. Then a man stands up in the rear of the plane. "I can make you feel like a real woman", he says. He's gorgeous: tall, built, with long, flowing black hair and jet black eyes. He starts to walk slowly up the aisle, unbuttoning his shirt one button at a time. >>>

43

>> No one moves. The woman is breathing heavily in anticipation as the stranger approaches. He removes his shirt. Muscles ripple across his chest as he reaches her, and extends the arm holding his shirt to the trembling woman, and whispers "Iron this".

Subject: Three Girlfriends

There is a man who has three girlfriends, but he does not know which one to marry. So he decides to give each one $5000 and see how they spend it.

The first one goes out and gets a total makeover with the money. She gets new clothes, a new hairdo, manicure, pedicure, the works, and tells the man, "I spent the money so I could look pretty for you because I love you so much."

The second one went and bought new golf clubs, a CD player, a television, and a stereo and gives them to the man. She says, "I bought these gifts for you with the money because I love you so much."

The third one takes the $5000 and invests it in the stock market, doubles her investment, returns the $5000 to the man and reinvests the rest. She says, "I am investing the rest of the money for our future because I love you so much."

The man thought long and hard about how each of the women spent the money. He finally decided to marry the one with the biggest tits.

Subject: Two Little Old Ladies

Two little old ladies were outside their nursing
home having a smoke — that's the only place they
could smoke at the nursing home — when it
started to rain. One of the ladies pulled out a
condom, cut off the end, put it over her cigarette,
and continued smoking.

The second old lady asks, "What's that?"
The first old lady replies, "A condom."
The second old lady then asks, "Where'd you get
it?" The first old lady replies, "You can get them
at any drugstore."

The next day the second old lady hobbles herself
into the local drugstore and announces to the
assistant that she wants a packet of condoms.
The guy looks at her kind of strangely — she is,
after all, in her 80s — but politely asks what brand
she prefers.

"Doesn't matter," she replies, "as long as it fits a
Camel."

Subject: The Koala Bear and The Hooker

A koala bear and a hooker go back to her place
and they get undressed. The koala bear goes down
on the hooker for three hours straight. She has
multiple orgasms. After three hours he stops, gets
up and puts on his clothes. The woman is hanging
back huffing and puffing with exhaustion. "Oh
God, that was great! Now I need my money."

The koala bear just looks at her and shrugs.
Then the hooker says, "No, I need my money. I'm
a hooker and this how I make a living."

The koala just looks at her and continues to put
on his clothes. The hooker gets up and and runs to
the bookshelf, grabs a dictionary and thumbs to
'hooker'. She hands it to the koala bear so he can
read: "Hooker: person who has sex for money."

The koala bear then turns the page to 'koala
bear' and walks out the door. The hooker reads:
"Koala Bear: eats bushes and leaves".

Subject: American tourist

An American touring Spain stopped at a local restaurant following a day of sightseeing. While sipping hsi sangria, he noticed a sizzling, scrumptious looking dish being served at the next table. Not only did it look good, the smell was wonderful. He asked the waiter, "What is that you just served?"

The waiter replied, "!Ah senor, you have excellent taste! Those are bulls testicles from the bull fight this morning. A delicacy!"

The American, though momentarily daunted, said, "What the hell, I'm on vacation! Bring me an order."

The waiter replied, "I am so sorry senor. There is only one serving per day because there is only one bull fight each morning. If you come early tomorrow and place your order, we will be sure to save you this delicacy."

The next morning, the American returned, placed his order, and then that evening he was served the one and only special delicacy of the day. After a few bites, and inspecting the contents of his plate, he called to the waiter and said, "These are delicious, but they are much, much smaller than the ones I saw your serve yesterday."

The waiter shrugged his shoulders and replied, "Si senor, sometimes the bull wins."

Subject: Safe sex

NB: Better when seen on the screen moving!

Subject: Afterlife

Doris missed her late husband Fred terribly. They had been married for over 40 years when Fred died suddenly. Fortunately Doris was left quite well off.

Sad and lonely, Doris took to visiting psychic healers and clairvoyants in the hope that she might be able to 'speak' to Fred just one more time. She had spent thousands of pounds of Fred's money to no avail, when she was recommended another clairvoyant whose seances had proved successful for others.

Paying her £100, Doris was shown into a darkened room, and a seat at a round table. The psychic went into a trance-like state and began calling to Fred: "Fred, are you out there? Can you hear me Fred? Doris is with me now and would like to speak to you."

This continued for some time, when suddenly a man's voice was heard in the room. Doris could not believe her ears, it was Fred's voice.   >>>

>>"Fred," she cried, "it's me, Doris. Can you hear me?"

"Hello Doris, how are you?" said the 'voice'.

"Oh, Fred, it's you! Are you all right? What do you do all day?"

"Well," said Fred, "it's like this: I get up and have sex, and then I have my breakfast, then I have a few more sessions of sex again, then I have lunch, followed by more sex, sometimes a siesta, then more sex before supper, and then I go to bed."

"Oh, oh, Fred, I had no idea Heaven was like that," wailed Doris.

"You were always a stupid woman, Doris. I'm a rabbit on Wimbledon Common."

Subject: Consulting wisdom

Last week I took some friends out to a restaurant and noticed that the waiter who took our order carried a spoon in his shirt pocket. It seemed a little strange, but I ignored it. However, when the bus-boy brought out water and utensils, I noticed he also had a spoon in his shirt pocket.

I then looked around the room and saw that all the waiters had a spoon in their pocket.

When the waiter came back to check on our order, I asked: "Why the spoon?"

"Well," he explained, "the restaurant's owners hired Andersen Consulting, experts in efficiency, in order to revamp all our procedures. After several months of statistical analysis, they concluded that customers drop their spoons 73.84% more often than any other utensil. This represents a drop frequency of approximately three spoons per table per hour. If our staff are prepared to deal with that contingency, we can reduce the >

>> number of trips back to the kitchen and save 1.5 man-hours per shift."

As we finished talking, a metallic sound was heard from behind me. Quickly, the waiter replaced the dropped spoon with the one in his pocket, and said: "I'll get another spoon next time I go to the kitchen instead of making an extra trip to get it right now."

I was rather impressed. The waiter continued taking our order and while my guests chose from the menu, I continued to look around. I then noticed that there was a very thin string hanging out of the waiter's fly. Looking around, I noticed that all the waiters had the same string hanging from their fly.

My curiosity got the better of me and before he walked off, I asked the waiter: "Excuse me, but can you tell me why you have that string right there?"

"Oh, certainly, " he answered, lowering his voice. "Not everyone is as observant as you. That   >>>

>> consulting firm I mentioned, also found out that we can save time in the toilet."

"How so?"

"See," he continued, "by tying this string to the tip of...you know...we can pull it out over the urinal without touching it and that way eliminate the need to wash the hands, shortening the time spent in the restroom by 76.39%."

"OK, that makes sense, but...if the string helps you get it out, how do you put it back in?"

"Well," he whispered, lowering his voice even further, "I don't know about the others, but I use the spoon."

Subject: Totally Sick! Urrrgggh....

Bob goes into the public restroom and sees this guy standing next to the urinal. The guy has no arms. As Bob's standing there, taking care of business, he wonders to himself how the poor slob is going to take a leak. Bob finishes and starts to leave when the man asks Bob to help him out. Being a kind soul, Bob says, "OK, sure I'll help you." The man asks, "Can you unzip my fly?" Bob says, "OK." Then the man says, "Can you pull it out for me?" Bob replies, "Uh, yeah, OK." Bob pulls it out and it has all kinds of mold and red bumps, with hair clumps, rashes, moles, scabs, scars, and reeks of something awful. Bob then shakes it, puts it back in and zips it up. the guy tells Bob, "Thanks man, I really appreciate it." Bob says, "No problem, but what the hell's wrong with your dick?"

The guy pulls his arms out of his shirt and says, "I don't know, but I sure ain't touching it."

Subject: Duck in a Pub

A duck went into a pub and took a seat at the bar. The publican said, "You're a Duck?!"

"That's right," said the duck, "I'd like a pint please."

"My God," exclaimed the publican, "You speak as well?!"

"Yes, that's right, I'm a talking duck. Could I have my pint please?"

The publican got talking to the duck who explained that he was working on a new building development just down the road. "I'll be around for a few weeks, so you'll be seeing me."

A few days later a tall man came into the pub and went up to the bar. The publican said, "I've not seen you around before, what brings you to these parts?" The man explained he was from the circus and they would be setting up the big top on the local green with performances every day for the>

>>next few weeks. The publican told him about his other customer: the talking duck. The man from the circus could not believe that the duck actually spoke. "I'd really like to meet this duck," he told the publican. "Do you suppose you could set up a meeting?"

The next day, when the duck came in for his usual, the publican told him about the circus that had come to town. "Do you know what I mean by a circus?" he asked the duck. "Yes, of course I know what a circus is,"said the duck.

"Well, they would really like to meet you, I think they would like you to work with them," said the publican.

"But what on earth would a circus want with a plasterer?" asked the duck.

Subject: A Sad Head

A man is waiting for his wife to give birth. The doctor comes and informs the dad that his son was born without torso, arms or legs. The son is just a head! But the dad loves his son and raises him as well as he can, with love and compassion.

After 21 years, the son is old enough for his first drink. Dad takes him to the bar and tearfully tells the son he is proud of him. Dad orders up the biggest, strongest drink for his boy on his 21st birthday. With all the bar patrons looking on curiously and the bartender shaking his head in disbelief, the boy takes his first sip of alcohol.. Swoooop! A torso pops out!

The bar is dead silent; then bursts into a whoop of joy. The father, shocked, begs his son to drink again. The patrons chant, "Take another drink!" The bartender shakes his head in disbelief. Swoooop! Two arms pop out of the new torso. The bar goes wild. The father, crying and wailing, begs his son to drink again. The patrons chant, "Take another drink!" The bartender is dismayed. By >

>> now the boy is getting tipsy, and with his new hands he reaches down, grabs his drink and guzzles the last of it. Swooooop! Two legs pop out. The bar is in chaos.

The father falls to his knees and tearfully thanks God. The boy stands up on his new legs and stumbles to the left...then to the right....right through the front door, into the street, where a truck runs him over and hills him instantly.

The bar falls silent. The father moans in grief. The bartender sighs and says, "That boy should have quit while he was a head."

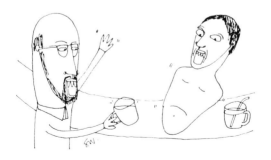

>>true stories or urban myths???

Subject: Actual letter sent to a bank

Apparently the bank thought it amusing enough to send to the New York Times.

Dear Sir,

I am writing to thank you for bouncing the cheque which I endeavoured to pay my plumber last month. By my calculations some three nanoseconds must have elapsed between his presenting the cheque and the arrival in my account of the funds needed to honour it. I refer, of course, to the automatic monthly deposit of my entire salary, an arrangement which, I admit, has only been in place for eight years. You are to be commended for seizing that brief window of opportunity, and also for debiting my account with $50 by way of penalty for the inconvenience I caused to your bank.

My thankfulness springs from the manner in which this incident has caused me to re-think >>

>>my errant financial ways. You have set me on
the path of fiscal righteousness. No more will our
relationship be blighted by these unpleasant
incidents, for I am restructuring my affairs in
1999, taking as my model the procedures, attitudes
and conduct of your very bank. I can think of no
greater compliment, and I know you will be
excited and proud to hear it.

To this end, please be advised about the following
changes:-

First, I have noticed that whereas I personally
attend to your telephone calls and letters, when I
try to contact you I am confronted by the
impersonal, ever-changing, pre-recorded, faceless
entity which your bank has become. From now on
I, like you, choose only to deal with a flesh and
blood person. My mortgage and loan repayments
will, therefore and hereafter, no longer be
automatic, but will arrive at your bank, by cheque,
addressed personally and confidentially to an
employee of your branch, whom you must
nominate. You will be aware that it is an offence
under the Postal Act for any other person to open>

> such an envelope. Please find attached an Application Contact Status which I require your chosen employee to complete. I am sorry it runs to eight pages, but in order that I know as much about him or her as your bank knows about me, there is no alternative. Please note that all copies of his or her medical history must be countersigned by a Justice of the Peace, and that the mandatory details of his/her financial situation (income, debts, assets and liabilities) must be accompanied by documented proof.

In due course I will issue your employee with a PIN number which he/she must quote in all dealings with me. I regret that it cannot be shorter than 28 digits, but — again — I have modelled it on the number of button presses required to access my account balance on your phone bank service. As they say, imitation is the sincerest form of flattery. Let me level the playing field even further by introducing you to my new telephone system, which you will notice, is very much like yours. My Authorised Contact at your bank — the only person with whom I will have any dealings >>

> — may call me at any time and will be answered by an automated voice. Press buttons as follows:

1. To make an appointment to see me
2. To query a missing repayment
3. To make a general complaint or enquiry
4. To transfer the call to my living room in case I am there. Extension of living room to be communicated at the time the call is received
5. To transfer the call to my bedroom in case I am sleeping. Extension of bedroom to be communicated at the time the call is received
6. To transfer the call to my toilet in case I am attending to nature. Extension of toilet to be communicated at the time the call is received
7. To transfer the call to my mobile phone in case I am not at home
8. To leave a message on my computer. To leave a message, a password to access my computer is required. Password will be communicated at a later date
9. To return to the main menu and listen carefully to options 1 through to 9

The contact will then be put on hold, pending the attention of my automated answering service. >

>>While this may, on occasion, involve a lengthy wait, uplifting music will play for the duration. This month I've chosen a refrain from The Best of Woody Guthrie:

> "Oh, the banks are made of marble
> With a guard at every door
> And the vaults are filled with silver
> That the miners sweated for"

After twenty minutes of that, our mutual contact will probably know it off by heart.

On a more serious note, we come to the matter of cost. As your bank has so often pointed out, the ongoing drive for greater efficiency comes at a cost — a cost which you have always been quick to pass on to me. Let me repay your kindness by passing some costs back. First, there is the matter of advertising material you send me. This I will read for a fee of $20 per page. Enquiries from your nominated contact will be billed at $5 per minute of my time spent in response. Any debits to my account, as, for example, in the matter of the penalty for the dishonoured cheque, will be >>

>passed back to you. My new phone service runs at 75 cents a minute (even Woody Guthrie doesn't come for free), so you would be well advised to keep your enquiries brief and to the point.

Regrettably, but again following your example, I must also levy an establishment fee to cover the setting up of this new arrangement.

May I wish you a happy, if ever-so-slightly less prosperous, New Year.

Your humble client.   **BANK**

Subject: It's The Navy

This is the transcript of an actual radio conversation recorded between a US Navy vessel and the Canadian authorities off Newfoundland in October 1995. The radio conversation was released by the Chief of Naval Operations 10/10/95.

Americans: Please divert your course 15 degrees to the north to avoid a collision.

Canadians: Recommend you divert YOUR course 15 degrees to the south to avoid a collision.

Americans: This is the Captain of a US Navy ship. I say again, divert YOUR course.

Canadians: No, I say again, divert YOUR course.

Americans: THIS IS THE AIRCRAFT CARRIER USS LINCOLN, THE SECOND LARGEST SHIP IN THE UNITED STATES' ATLANTIC FLEET. WE ARE ACCOMPANIED BY THREE DESTROYERS AND THREE CRUISERS. I DEMAND THAT YOU CHANGE YOUR COURSE 15 DEGREES NORTH, THAT'S ONE-FIVE DEGREES NORTH, OR COUNTER MEASURES WILL BE UNDERTAKEN TO ENSURE THE SAFETY OF THIS VESSEL.

Canadians: This is a lighthouse. Your call.

Subject: Dealing With The Irate Customer

For all of you out there who've had to deal with an irate customer, this one is for you. It's a classic, in tribute to those 'special' customers we all love.

An award should go to the United Airlines gate agent in Denver for being smart and funny, and making her point, when confronted with a passenger who probably deserved to fly as cargo.

A crowded United flight was cancelled. A single agent was rebooking a long line of inconvenienced travellers. Suddenly an angry passenger pushed his way to the desk. He slapped his ticket down on the counter and said, "I HAVE to be on this flight and it has to be FIRST CLASS."

The agent replied, "I'm sorry sir. I'll be happy to try to help you, but I've got to help these folks first. If you will just get back in line I'm sure we'll be able to work something out when it's your turn.">

>>The passenger was unimpressed. He asked loudly, so that the passengers behind him could hear, "Do you have any idea who I am?"

Without hesitating, the gate agent smiled and grabbed her public address microphone. "May I have your attention please? We have a passenger here at the gate WHO DOES NOT KNOW WHO HE IS. If anyone can help him find his identity, please come to the gate."

With the folks behind him laughing hysterically, the man glared at the agent, gritted his teeth and swore, "F*** you!"

Without flinching, she smiled and said, "I'm sorry, sir, but you'll have to stand in line for that, too."

Subject: Bank Robbery

Excerpt from an article about a bank robbery which appeared in the Dublin Times (Metropolitan Edition, page 2) on 2 March 1999:

Once inside the bank, shortly after midnight, their efforts at disabling the internal security system got underway immediately. The robbers, who expected to find one or two large safes filled with cash and valuables, were surprised to see hundreds of smaller safes scattered throughout the bank.

The robbers cracked the first safe's combination, and inside they found only a bowl of vanilla pudding. As recorded on the bank's audiotape system, one said, "At least we'll get a bit to eat."

The robbers opened up a second safe, and it also contained nothing but vanilla pudding. The process continued until all the safes were opened. They found not one pound sterling, not a diamond, or an ounce of gold. Instead, all the safes contained covered bowls of pudding.

Disappointed, the robbers made a quiet exit, each leaving with nothing more than a queasy, uncomfortably full stomach.

>>>>>>Scroll down to next page

>>>>>>
>>>>>>
>>>>>>
>>>>>>The newspaper headline read:
IRELAND'S LARGEST SPERM BANK
ROBBED EARLY THIS MORNING.

Subject: Questions most feared by men

1. What are you thinking about?
2. Do you love me?
3. Do I look fat?
4. Do you think she is prettier than me?
5. What would you do if I died?

What makes these questions so difficult is that every one is guaranteed to explode into a major argument if the man answers incorrectly (ie. tells the truth). Therefore, as a public service, each question is analysed below, along with possible responses.

Question 1: What are you thinking about?
The proper answer to this, of course, is: "I'm sorry if I have been pensive, dear. I was just reflecting on what a warm, wonderful, thoughtful, caring, intelligent woman you are, and how lucky I am to have met you." This response obviously bears no resemblance to the true answer, which most likely is one of the following:
a) Baseball
b) Football

c) How fat you are
d) How much prettier she is than you
e) How I would spend the insurance money if you died.

Question 2: *Do you love me?*

The proper response is: "YES!" or, if you feel a more detailed answer is in order, "Yes, dear." Inappropriate responses include:
a) Oh Yeah, shit loads
b) Would it make you feel better if I said yes?
c) That depends on what you mean by love
d) Does it matter?
e) Who, me?

Question 3: *Do I look fat?*

The correct answer is an emphatic: "Of course not!" Among the incorrect answers are: Compared to what?
a) I wouldn't call you fat, but you're not exactly think
b) A little extra weight looks good on you
c) I've seen fatter

d) Could you repeat the question? I was just wondering how I would spend the insurance money if you died.

Question 4: Do you think she's prettier than me?

Once again, the proper response is an emphatic: "Of course not!" Incorrect responses include:
a) Yes, but you have a better personality
b) Not prettier, but definitely thinner
c) Not as pretty as you when you were her age
d) Define 'pretty'?
e) Could you repeat the question? I was just wondering how I would spend the insurance money if you died.

Question 5: What would you do if I died?

A definite no-win question. (The real answer, of course, is "Buy a Corvette and a boat." Now matter how you answer this, be prepared for at least an hour of follow up questions, usually along these lines:

Woman:	Would you get married again?
Man:	Definitely not!

Woman:	Why not? don't you like being married?
Man:	Of course I do.
Woman:	Then why wouldn't you remarry?
Man:	OK, I'd get married again.
Woman:	You would? (With a hurtful look on her face.)
Woman:	Would you sleep with her in our bed?
Man:	Where else would we sleep?
Woman:	Would you put away my pictures, and replace them with pictures of her?
Man:	That would seem like the proper thing to do.
Woman:	And would you let her use my golf clubs?
Man:	No, she plays tennis.
Woman:	---------------- silence --------------
Man:	Oh shit.

>>how to succeed in business

Subject: Excelling in meetings

Bored during meetings? Why not try some of these neat little exercises. Not only willl it make meetings more interesting, but your colleagues will become suddenly more alert and maintain a respectful distance.

During a meeting:

1. Discreetly clasp hold of someone's hand and whisper, "Can you feel it?" from the corner of your mouth.
2. Draw enormous genitalia on your notepad and show it to the person next to you for their approval.
3. When refreshments are presented, immediately distribute half a biscuit to each of the attendees.
4. Wear a hands-free phone headset throughout. Once in a while drift off into an unrelated conversation, such as, "I don't care if there are no dwarfs, just get the show done!"

5. Write the words "he fancies you" on your pad and show it to the person next to you while indicating with your pen.

6. Respond to a serious question with, "I don't know what to say, obviously I'm flattered, but it's all happened so fast."

7. Use Nam-style jargon such as "what's the ETA?", "who's on recon?" and "Charlie don't surf".

8. Reconstruct the meeting in front of you using Action Man figures. When anyone moves re-arrange the figures accordingly.

9. Draw a chalk circle around one of the chairs then avoid sitting on it when the meeting starts. When someone does eventually sit in it, cover your mouth and gasp.

10. Turn your back on the meeting and sit facing the window with your legs stretched out. Announce that you "love this dirty town".

11. Walk directly up to a colleague and stand noes to nose with him for one minute.

12. Reflect sunlight into everyone's eyes from your watch face.

13. Repeat every idea they express in a baby voice while moving your hand like a chattering mouth.
14. Hum 'We'll meet again' throughout.
15. Drop meaningless and confusing management speak into conversations, such as: "What's the margin, Marvin?" "When's this turkey going to get basted?" "If we don't get this brook babbling we're all going to end up looking like doe-eyed labradors"
16. Use a large hunting knife to point at your visual aids.
17. Announce that you've run off some copies of the meeting agenda. Then hand out pieces of paper that read: 'My Secret Agenda. i) Trample the week. ii) Triumph alone. iii) Invade Poland.
18. When referring to someone in the room, always call them your 'homey'.
19. Leave long pauses in your speech at random moments. When someone is prompted to interject, shout "I AM NOT FINISHED".

Subject: Business efficiency or Schubert's Unfinished

The president of a large company invited his team of experts who dealt with improving the company's efficiency to a concert. It was Schubert's Unfinished Symphony. The team felt obliged to report to the president on the concert, and being concerned with efficiency, they made the following recommendations:

1. For considerable periods, the four oboe players had nothing to do. Their number should be reduced and their work spread over the whole orchestra.
2. Forty violins were playing identical notes. This seems an unnecessary duplication, and this section should be drastically cut. If a larger volume of sound was required, this could be achieved through an elecronic amplifier.
3. Much effort was absorbed in the playing of dem/semi-quavers. This seems an excessive refinement, and it is recommended that all notes be rounded to the nearest demi-quaver.>

>> if this were done, it should be possible to use trainees and lower-grade operators.

4. No useful purpose is served by repeating with horns the passage that has already been handled by the strings. If all such redundant passages were eliminated, the concert could be reduced to twenty minutes.

If Schubert had attended to these matters he probably would have been able to finish his symphony after all...

79

Subject: How not to fall asleep in meetings

Do you keep falling asleep in meetings?
Here's something to change all that....

BULLSHIT BINGO

How to play: simply check off 5 words/phrases in one meeting and shout out BINGO!
It's that easy!

SYNERGY	MOVERS AND SHAKERS
TAKE THAT OFF LINE	BALL PARK
STRATEGIC FIT	PROACTIVE, NOT REACTIVE
AT THE END OF THE DAY	WIN WIN SITUATION
GAP ANAYLSIS	THINK OUTSIDE THE BOX
BEST PRACTICE	FAST TRACK
THE BOTTOM LINE	EMPOWER EMPLOYEES
CORE BUSINESS	NO BLAME
LESSONS LEARNED	STRETCH THE ENVELOPE
TOUCH BASE	REVISIT
KNOWLEDGE BASE	RESULTS DRIVEN
GAME PLAN	TOTAL QUALITY
BAND WIDTH	SLIPPERY SLOPE
HARDBALL	MINDSET
OUT OF THE LOOP	PUT THIS ONE TO BED
GO THE EXTRA MILE	CLIENT FOCUSED
BENCHMARK	QUALITY DRIVEN
THE BIG PICTURE	MOVE THE GOAL POSTS
VALUE ADDED	

Testimonials from players:

"I had only been in the meeting for 5 minutes when I yelled Bingo!"

"My attention span at meetings has improved dramatically."

"It's a wheeze, metings will never the same for me after my first outright win."

"The atmosphere was tense at the loast process workshop as 32 of us listened intently for the elusive 5th."

"The facilitator was gob-smacked as we all screamed bingo for the 3rd time in 2 hours."

"I feel the game has enchanced the overall quality of meetings per se on a quid pro quo basis."

"People are now even listening to mumblers and bores, thanks to Bullshit Bingo."

"Bonza! You could have cut the atmosphere with a cricket stump as we waited for the 5th delivery."

Subject: Women only

*For those cultivating their "Inner Bitch" here is a
new and improved list.*

1. Do I look like a God-damn people person?
2. I can please only one person per day. Today is
   not your day; tomorrow isn't looking good
   either.
3. This isn't an office. It's hell with fluorescent
   lighting.
4. I started out with nothing and I still have most
   of it left.
5. I pretend to work. They pretend to pay me.
6. Sarcasm is just one more service we offer.
7. If I throw a stick, will you leave?
8. If I want to hear the pitter patter of little feet,
   I'll put shoes on my cats.
9. Does your train of thought have a caboose?
10. Errors have been made. Others will be blamed.
11. And your cry-baby, whiny-assed opinion would
    be...?
12. A PBS mind in an MTV world.   >>

13. Allow me to introduce my selves.
14. Whatever kind of look you were going for, you missed.
15. Suburbia --- where they tear out the trees and then name streets after them.
16. Well, this day was a total waste of makeup.
17. Are those your eyeballs? I found them in my cleavage.
18. I'm not your type. I'm not inflatable.
19. Not all men are annoying. Some are dead.
20. Did I mention the kick in the groin you'll be receiving if you touch me?
21. A woman's favourite position is CEO.
22. I'm trying to imagine you with a personality.
23. Stress is when you wake up screaming and your realise you haven't fallen asleep yet.
24. Too many freaks, not enough circuses.
25. Macho Law prohibits me from admitting I'm wrong.
26. Nice perfume. Must you marinate in it?
27. Chaos, panic, and disorder----my work here is done.
28. I plead contemporary insanity.
29. How do I set a laser printer to stun?
30. Meandering to a different drummer.

31. I love deadlines. I especially like the whooshing sound they make as the go flying by.
32. Am I getting smart with you? How would you know?
33. I'd explain it to you, but your brain would explode.
34. Tell me what you need, and I'll tell you how to get along without it.
35. Accept that some days you're the pigeon, and some days you're the statue.
36. Needing someone is like needing a parachute. If he isn't there the first time you need him, chances are you won't be needing him again.
37. I don't have an attitude problem. You have a perception problem.
38. I don't suffer from stress. I'm a carrier.

Subject: Nova Awards

These are the nominees for the Chevy Nova Award. This is given out in Honor of General Motor's fiasco in trying to market this car in Central and south America. "No va" means, of course, in Spanish, "it doesn't go".

1. The Dairy Association's huge success with the campaign "Got Milk?" prompted them to expand advertising to Mexico. It was soon brought to their attention the Spanish translation read "Are you lactating?"
2. Coors put its slogan, "Turn It Loose" into Spanish, where it was read as "Suffer from Diarrhoea".
3. Scandinavian vacuum manufacturer, Electrolux, used the following in an American campaign: "Nothing sucks like an Electrolux".
4. Clairol introuced the "Mist Stick", a curling tong, into Germany, only to find out that "Mist" is slang for manure.
5. When Gerber started selling baby food in Africa, they used the same packaging as in the US, with the smiling baby on the label. Later

they learned that in Africa, companies routinely put pictures on the labels to show what's inside, since many people cannot read.

6. Colgate introduced a toothpaste in France called Cue, the name of a notorious porn magazine.

7. An American t-shirt maker in Miami printed shirts for the Spanish market which promoted the Pope's visit. Instead of "I saw the Pope" (el Papa), the shirts read "I saw the Potato" (la papa).

8. Pepsi's "Come Alive with the Pepsi Generation" translated into "Pepsi Brings Your Ancestors Back From the Grave" in Chinese.

9. The Coca-Cola name in China was first read as "Kekoukela", meaning "Bite the wax tadpole" or "female horse stuffed with wax", depending on the dialect. Coke then researched 40,000 characters to find a phonetic equivalent "kokoukole", translating into "happiness in the mouth".

10. Frank Perdue's chicken slogan, "It takes a strong man to make a tender chicken" was translated into Spanish as "it takes an aroused man to make chicken affectionate".

11. When Parker Pen marketed a ball-point pen in Mexico, its ads were supposed to have read, "It won't leak in your pocket and embarrass you". The company thought the word 'embarazar' (to impregnate) meant to embarrass, so the ad read: "It won't leak in your pocket and make you pregnant!"

12. When American Airlines wanted to advertise its new leather first class seats in the Mexican market, it translated its "Fly In Leather" campaign literally, which meant "Fly Naked" (vuela en cuero) in Spanish. (This one probably worked out OK!)

Subject: Those lists! On Cows and Politics

FEUDALISM: You have two cows. Your lord takes some of the milk.

FACISM: You have two cows. The government takes both, hires you to take care of them, and sells you the milk.

COMMUNISM: You have two cows. You have to take care of the, but the government takes all the milk.

DICTATORSHIP: You have two cows. The government takes both and shoots you.

NIGERIAN DEMOCRACY: You have two cows. The government takes both, shoots you and sends the cows to Zurich.

MILTARISM: You have two cows. The government takes both and drafts you.

SINGAPOREAN DEMOCRACY: You have two cows. the government fines you for keeping two unlicensed farm animals in an apartment.

AMERICAN DEMOCRACY: The government promises to give you two cows if you vote for it. After the election, the President is impeached for speculating in cow futures. The press dubs the affair "Cowgate". The cow sues you for breach of contract.

BRITISH DEMOCRACY: You have two cows. You feed them sheep's brains and they go mad. The government doesn't do anything.

EUROPEAN DEMOCRACY: You have two cows. At first the government regulates what you can feed them and when you can milk them. Then it pays you to milk them. After that it takes both, shoots one, milks the other and pours the milk down the drain. Then it requires you to fill out forms for the missing cows.

CAPITALISM: You have two cows. You sell one and buy a bull.

HONG KONG CAPITALISM: You have two cows. You sell three of them to your publicly-listed company, using letters of credit opened by your brother-in-law at the bank, then you execute a debt/equity swap with an associated general offer so that you get all four cows back, with a tax deduction for keeping five cows. The milk rights of six cows are transferred via a Panamanian intermediary to a Cayman Islands company secretly owned by the majority shareholder, who sells the right all seven cows' milk back to the listed company. The annual report says that the company owns eight cows, with an option on one more. Meanwhile, you kill the two cows because of bad feng shui.

HINDUISM: You have two cows. You give them all your food.

TOTALITARIANISM: You have two cows. The government takes them and denies they ever existed. Milk is banned.

POLITICAL CORRECTNESS: You are associated with (the concept of 'ownership' is a symbol of the phallocentric, warmongering, intolerant past) two differently aged (but no less valuable to society) bovines of non-specified gender.

COUNTERCULTURE: Wow, dude, there's like....these two cows, man! You have *got* to have some of this milk!

SURREALISM: You have two giraffes. The government requires you to take harmonica lessons.

Subject: Prayers

The Girlies' Prayer

Our Marks
Which art with Spencers
hallowed be thy foodhall
Thy Gucci watch
Thy Fendi bag
In Hermes
As it is in Harrods
Give us each day our Visa Gold
And forgive us our overdraft
As we forgive those who stop our Next Card
And lead us not into dorothy Perkins
And deliver us from Topshop
For thine is the Naff Naff, the Cartier and the
Versace
For Gaultier and Eternity.
AMEX

The Lads' Prayer

Our beer,
Which art in barrels,
Hallowed be thy drink.
Thy will be drunk,
I will be drunk,
At home as it is in the local.
Forgive us this day our daily spillage
As we forgive those who spillest against us.
And lead us not into the practice of poncey wine
tasting,
And deliver us from alco-pops,
For mine is the bitter,
The ale and the lager,
Forever and ever;
BARMEN.

93

>>something for Christmas

Subject: The Twelve Days of Christmas

14th December
My Dearest Darling John,
I went to the door today and the postman had delivered a Partridge in a Pear Tree. What a delightful gift. Thank you, Darling, for the lovely thought.
With deep love and affection always,
Your loving Agnes.

15th December
My Dearest John,
Today the postman brought your very sweet Two Turtle Doves. I am delighted. They are adorable.
All my love forever, Agnes.

16th December
Dearest John,
Oh, how extravagant you are. I really must protest. I don't deserve such generosity. Three French hens. I insist you are too kind.
My love, Agnes.

17th December

Dear John,

What can I say? Four Calling Birds arrived this morning with the postman.

Your kindness is too much.

Love, Agnes.

18th December

Dearest John,

What a surprise. Today the postman delivered Five Gold Rings, one for each finger. You really are an impossible boy, but I love you.

Frankly all the birds are beginning to squawk and are getting on my nerves.

Your loving Agnes.

19th December

Dear John

When I opened the door this morning there were actually Six bloody great Geese Laying Eggs all over the front step. What on earth do you think I can do with them all?

The neighbours are beginning to smell the birds and I cannot sleep. Please STOP sending them.

Agnes.

20th December

John,

What is it with you and these sodding birds? Now I get Seven Swans a Swimming. Is it some sort of Goddamned Joke? The house is full of bird shit and it is not funny anymore.

Stop sending these bloody birds.

Agnes.

21st December

OK Buster,

I think I prefer the birds. What the hell am I going to do with eight Maids-a-Milking? It's enough with all those bloody birds and now I have eight cows shitting all over the house and mooing all night.

Lay off, Agnes.

22nd December

LOOK CRAPHEAD

What are you? some kind of nut? Now I have Nine Pipers Playing and Christ, do they play!!! When they aren't playing their sodding pipes, they are chasing the maids through the cow shit. The cows keep mooing and trampling all over the bloody birds and the neighbours are threatening to have me evicted.

Get knotted, Agnes.

23rd December

YOU ROTTEN BASTARD

Now I have Ten Ladies Dancing. How on earth can you call these whores "ladies" is beyond me. They are pulling the Pipers all nightlong, the cows can't sleep and have diarrhoea. My living room is a sea of shit and the landlord has just declared the building as unfit for human habitation.

Piss Off, Agnes.

24th December

LISTEN SHITFACE

What with the Eleven Lords Leaping all over the maids and me, I shall never walk again. The Pipers are fighting the Lords for crumpet and committing sodomy with the cows. The birds are all dead and rotting, having been trampled on during the orgy. I hope you are satisfied, you swine.

Your sworn enemy, Agnes.

25th December

YOU STINKING LOUSY SHIT

Twelve Drummers have teamed up with the Pipers and are making one hell of a bleeding din. Both lots have begun buggering the Lords as well as the cows and Christ know's what's happened to the Milkmaids. They've probably drowned in the cow shit by now. The only way I've saved myself from being screwed to death is by hiding up that sodding Pear Tree which has been so well fertilised by shit that it has grown through the bloody roof.

FUCK OFF, Agnes.

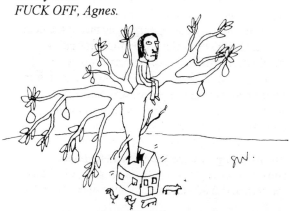

Subject: George the Postie

It was George's last day on the job as a postman after 35 years of delivering the mail through all kinds of weather to the same neighbourhood. When he arrived at the first house on his route George was greeted by the whole family who congratulated him and sent him on his way with a tidy gift of $100.

At the second house the owners presented him with a box of fine Cuban cigars. The folks at the third house, knowing he was a keen fisherman, handed him a selection of terrific fishing lures.

At the fourth house George was met at the door by a strikingly beautiful woman in a revealing negligee. She took him by the hand, beckoning him in, closing the door behind them, leading him up the stairs to the bedroom where she proceeded to blow his mind with the most passionate love he had ever experienced.

When he had had enough, they went downstairs, where she then fixed him a giant breakfast: eggs, potatoes, ham, sausage, blueberry waffles, and fresh-squeezed orange juice. When>>

>>he was truly satisfied she poured him a cup of steaming fresh coffee.

As she was pouring, he noticed a dollar bill sticking out on the saucer from under the cup. "All this was just too wonderful for words," he said, "but what's the dollar for?"

"Well," she said, "last night I told my husband that today would be your last day, and that we should do something special for you. I asked him what to give you. He said, "Screw him. Give him a dollar. The breakfast was my idea.""

Subject: First Mass

A new priest at his first mass was so nervous he could hardly speak. After mass he asked the monsignor how he had done. The monsignor replied, "When I am worried about getting nervous on the pulpit, I put a glass of vodka next to the water jug. If I start to get nervous, I take a sip."

So next Sunday the new priest took the monsignor's advice. At the beginning of the sermon, he got nervous and took a drink. He proceeded to talk up a storm, with frequent sips as the sermon progressed.

Upon his return to his office after mass, he found following note on the door:

>>Sip the vodka, don't gulp.
>>There are 10 commandments, not 12.
>>There are 12 disciples, not 10.
>>Jesus was consecrated, not constipated.
>>Jacob wagered his donkey, he did not bet his ass.
>>We do not refer to Jesus Christ as the late JC.

>>The Father, Son and Holy Ghost are not referred to as Daddy-O, Laddy-O and the Spook.

>>David slew Goliath; he did not kick the shit out of him.

>>When David was hit by a rock and knocked off his donkey, don't say he was stoned off his ass.

>>We do not refer to the cross as the "Big T".

>>When Jesus broke the bread at the Last Supper He said, "Take this and eat it for it is my body". He did not say, "Eat me."

>>The Virgin Mary is not called "Mary with the Cherry".

>>The recommended grace before a meal is not: "Rub-A-Dub-Dub thanks for the grub, yeah God!"

>>Next sunday there will be a taffy-pulling contest at St Peters, not a Peter-pulling contest at St Taffy's.

Subject: The Laboratory Rabbit

One fine sunny morning a brown and white rabbit
managed to escape from his cage in the laboratory.
He hopped across the carpark unnoticed and burrowed
under the hedge. On the other side, he found himself in
a vast field of grass. Another older rabbit came up and
introduced himself. "You're new around here, where
have you come from?"

The rabbit explained how he had managed to escape
from the laboratory where he had been born. The older
rabbit said, "It sounds as if you've got a lot of catching
up to do. All the grass is free for eating. The next field
is full of tender young carrots — all for eating. Over
that grassy mound you will find the female rabbits and
they will be so happy to meet you."

The rabbit could not believe how wonderful it all was.
He ate and ate; he met the female rabbits and copulated
frantically until he was exhausted and lay down under
the hedge for a rest.

He was awoken by the older rabbit who said, "Well,
how did you like your first day of freedom?"   >>>

>>"It was unbelievable," answered the laboratory rabbit, "the best day of my life, but now I must be getting back."

"Why on earth would you be returning to your cage?" exclaimed the older rabbit.

"I'm desperate for a cigarette."

Subject: Strip Club

An Englishman, Irishman and Scotsman go to a strip club. They shove up to the front row and the stripper does her stuff. For the finale she waggles her naked bum in the Englishman's face. He reaches for his wallet, takes out a tenner, licks it and slaps it on her left buttock.

The stripper moves along and repeats her bumps and grinds in front of the Irishman. He too takes a tenner from his wallet, licks it and slaps it on her right cheek.

She now confronts the Scot with her arse and wiggles it as before. He also removes his wallet, takes out his credit card, swipes it and takes £20 cash back....

Subject: Using logic

Two builders (Jim and Steve) are seated either side of a table in a rough pub when a well-dressed man enters, orders a beer and sits on a stool at the bar. The two builders start to speculate about the occupation of the Suit.

Jim: I reckon he's an accountant.
Steve: No way, he's a stockbroker.
Jim: He ain't no stockbroker! A stockbroker wouldn't come in here!

The argument continues for some time until the volume of beer gets the better of Jim and he makes for the toilet. On entering, he sees the Suit standing at a urinal. Curiosity and several beers spur the builder to enquire...

Jim: Scuse me... no offence meant, but me and me mate were wondering what you do for a living?
Suit: No offence taken! I'm a Logical Scientist by profession.
Jim: Oh! What's that then?
Suit: I'll try to explain by example... Do you have a goldfish at home?
Jim: Er... mmm... well yeah, I do as it happens.
Suit: Well, it's logical to follow that you keep in in a bowl or in a pond. Which is it? >>>

>>

Jim: It's in a pond.

Suit: Well, it's reasonable to suppose that you have a large garden then?

Jim: As it happens, yes I have got a big garden.

Suit: Well then, it's logical to assume that in this town if you have a large garden, you also have a large house?

Jim: As it happens I've got a five bedroom house... built it myself!

Suit: Well, given that you've built a five bedroom house, it is logical to assume that you haven't built it just for yourself and that you are quite probably married?

Jim: Yes, I am married, I live with my wife and three children.

Suit: Well then, it is logical to assume that you are sexually active with your wife on a regular basis?

Jim: Yep, four nights a week!

Suit: Then it is logical to assume that you do not masturbate very often?

Jim: Me? Never!

Suit: Well there you are! That's Logical Science at work.

Jim: How's that then?

Suit: Well, from finding out that you have a goldfish, I've told you about the size of your garden, the size of your house, your family and your sex life!

Jim: I see! That's pretty impressive... thanks mate.

Both leave the toilet and Jim returns to his mate. >>>

>>

Steve: I see the Suit was in there. Did you ask him what he does for a living?

Jim: Yep! He's a Logical Scientist.

Steve: What's that then?

Jim: I'll try and explain. Do you have a goldfish?

Steve: Nope.

Jim: Well then, you're a wanker.

108

Subject: Three construction workers

Three friends — an Englishman, an Irishman and an Italian man — worked on a building site right up on the 32nd floor. They looked forward eagerly to relaxing over their lunchbreak.

One Monday morning the Englishman went to open his lunch box, remarking "I wonder what my sandwiches will be today? All last week it was ham and I am fed up!" He was really pissed off to find it was ham again! "So help me, if I get ham tomorrow, I will kill myself...", he swore.

The Italian man opened his lunch box, telling the others that he had had salami in his sandwiches every day for the past 10 days. He peered into his box, only to shout, "Mama Mia, eeet's the salami AGAIN!!! If I get it tomorrow I will top myself!"

The Irishman, following the example set by his friends, opened up his lunchbox, saying that he had had cheese in his sandwiches for weeks and was fed up. It was cheese again! "Sweet Mother of Mary, I smell the cheese. I swear I will kill myself if I see cheese again this week."

The next day, the three sat down on the steps of the crane for their lunchbreak. They all opened their lunchboxes together, and as each man saw the contents of their sandwiches, they threw themselves over the edge to their deaths.   >>>

>>>At the inquest, the coroner spoke to the deceased men's wives. He asked the Englishman's wife had she known how depressed her husband had been at the monotony of his ham-sandwich lunch? Sobbing, the wife replied that she'd no idea. She said she would have given him smoked salmon sandwiches if that could bring him back to her.

The coroner asked the Italian wife the same question. Weeping and wailing, she said she thought salami was her husband's favourite and that is why she always gave him salami sandwiches.

The coroner then turned to the Irishman's wife. "Oh, Your Honour, if only I'd known," she said, "but, for sure, he always made his own sandwiches."

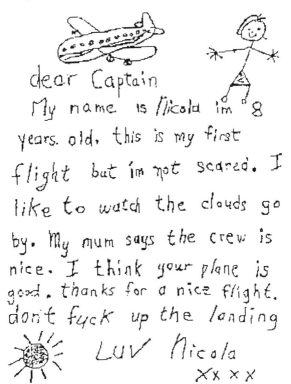

dear Captain

My name is Nicola im 8 years. old, this is my first flight but im not scared. I like to watch the clouds go by. My mum says the crew is nice. I think your plane is good. thanks for a nice flight. dont fuck up the landing

LUV Nicola

xx xx

Subject: Shipwrecked

>A guy, a sheep, and a dog were the only survivors of a terrible shipwreck. They found themselves stranded on a desert island. After being there awhile, they got into the habit of going to the beach every evening to watch the sunset.

>One particular evening, the sky was red with beautiful cirrus clouds, the breeze was warm and gentle; a perfect night for romance. As they stood there, the sheep started looking better and better to the man.

>Soon, he leaned over to the sheep and put his arm around her. The dog got jealous, growling fiercely until the man took his arm from around the sheep.

>After that, the three continued to enjoy the sunsets together, but there was no more cuddling.

>A few weeks passed, and lo and behold, there was another shipwreck. The only survivor was a beautiful young woman---the most beautiful woman the guy had ever seen. She was in a pretty bad way when they rescued her, and slowly they nursed her back to health.

>When the young woman was well enough, they introduced her to their evening beach sunset ritual. It was a perfect night for romance and pretty soon the guy started to get "those feelings" again. He fought them as long as he could, but finally gave in. Cautiously he leaned over to the young woman, and whispered in her ear..."Would you mind taking the dog for a walk?"